EVERYDAY HAIKU
AN ANTHOLOGY

KRISTEN RINGMAN
Editor

WANDERING MUSE PRESS
LEE, NH
USA

COPYRIGHT

Everyday Haiku: an anthology
Copyright © 2017 by Kristen Ringman

Editor: Kristen Ringman
Associate Editor: Carrie Nassif
Assistant Editors: Marsha Pincus and Pam Helberg
Editorial Consultant: Nicole Galland

Cover Design: Mona Z. Kraculdy
Cover Photos: Kristen Ringman

Please address inquiries to the publisher:

Wandering Muse Press
wanderingmusepress@gmail.com
https://followthewanderingmuse.com/ wandering-muse-press/

Printed in the United States of America

ISBN-13: 978-0998451701
ISBN-10: 0998451703

A First Wandering Muse Press Edition

CONTENTS

INTRODUCTION   7
by KRISTEN RINGMAN

**INSTRUCTIONS FOR CREATING THE HAIKU
ROOM**   9
by NICOLE GALLAND

January   11

February   18

March   31

April   36

May   43

June   49

July   56

August   64

September   72

October   76

November   84

December   93

CONTRIBUTORS   101

INTRODUCTION

by KRISTEN RINGMAN

This book began with the decision of a handful of writers to write a haiku every day for one full year back in 2014. These writers came together and shared their poems in a Facebook group called The Haiku Room, begun and initially administrated by Nicole Galland. I joined the group myself early on, encouraged by the passion of women writers I knew through an organization called AROHO (A Room of Her Own Foundation). The Haiku Room also branched out to male writers, though there remain a handful of AROHO women at its core. Pam Helberg is now the group administrator.

To give some background on the form: traditionally, a haiku is a Japanese poem of seventeen syllables organized into three lines of five, seven, and five. It tends to evoke images of the natural world, but our group occasionally played with the content while trying to remain true to the short form itself.

At the end of 2014, the over two hundred members of the group all agreed that putting together an anthology of our first year together sounded wonderful. Since we were a community of encouragers, we also decided that everyone who submitted to this anthology would get at least one haiku of theirs published inside it. I volunteered to be the gatherer of haiku and the publisher of this venture, because I've always wanted to edit an anthology and understand the work involved in publishing firsthand. I had also just started a website for writers who travel called Follow the Wandering Muse and a Wandering Muse Press was an easy and fitting addition.

Doing this work has been such a great experience and these haiku are as raw as they are beautiful and surprising. I hope you find inspiration in these shards of people's lives, whether they motivate you to write your own or help you appreciate what happens when you only have seventeen syllables to cut out a piece of your personal truth and share it with the world. To stay true to the spirit of The Haiku Room, these haiku have been organized carefully by seasonal themes.

INSTRUCTIONS FOR CREATING THE HAIKU ROOM

by NICOLE GALLAND

1. In college, be truculent and ornery, and have a wretched experience writing your undergraduate honors dissertation on "the religio-aesthetics of Basho's haiku." Graduate with a mild aversion to haiku; become a writer of lengthy novels, perhaps as a "who needs you?" retort to Basho. Allow at least 20 years to pass.

2. While going through a divorce, go to Haiti after a devastating earthquake. Volunteer to help at a rural medical clinic, with no qualifications beyond good intentions. Befriend some nurses who actually know what they are doing.

3. After 10 days, return home to the United States and immediately lose touch with all the nurses, except for one you maintain a very passing Facebook connection to. Allow at least 3 years to pass. Get married again and stuff.

4. One day, notice that the nurse has started to write and post a daily haiku – really good ones. Feel inspired by the daily meditative discipline of this. Decide this practice is perfect for you at this moment in your life.

5. Since it's already December, commit to writing one haiku a day for the following calendar year.

6. Remember that you are terribly undisciplined about doing things on your own, but stellar about doing them when other people are counting on you. Wonder if maybe other

writers would like to undertake this practice with you, in a manner that would hold you accountable.

7. Reach out to writers you know, especially (but not exclusively) the women you met at a recent retreat held by AROHO (A Room Of Her Own Foundation). Explain that you want to somehow do this "year of haiku" via social media (= best way to ensure accountability given geographical challenges).

8. Be delighted when 6 then 12 then 18 people sign on before January 1. Be delighted when somebody suggests, and then arranges, a private Facebook Group so that you can all share haiku with each other but not with the world at large. Be delighted when somebody dubs this "The Haiku Room." Be delighted when somebody contributes beautiful art for the cover image. Be delighted when the people who committed to the Haiku Room reach out to their friends who reach out to their friends who reach out to their friends.

9. Less than three months in, be absolutely gobsmacked that there are now more than 200 members of the Haiku Room. (Including the nurse!)

10. Write (pretty much) a haiku a day for 365 days and post to the Room. Read others' haiku. Swoon over many of them. Learn other writers' style; their life events; in some ways, their souls. Feel profound gratitude for their generosity, skill, depth, humor, insight, and mischief.

(CODA: 11. Read Basho for the first time in 20-odd years, and love him as much as you did before you started writing a dissertation about him.)

January

beginnings

Fear is eating me
for breakfast, lunch, and dinner.
Must stop feeding it.

Jennifer Steil

Sturdy, wooden, vast,
my desk has expectations.
I work on the floor.

Jennifer Steil

Caged bird calls brightly
creating each day afresh
light as a feather.

Jennifer Newsome

Among other bird
songs: *stor-ies, stor-ies, stor-ies.*
And the day begins.

Pete Follansbee

I ache from beauty
bold for which there are no words
only poetry

Mary Pecaut

Unwritten haiku:
they sit in my heart like an
ache, a song unsung.

Lisa Lutwyche

it's a bit like this —
stray thoughts wrap around my brain
squeeze out poetry

Liz Boquet

The center does not
hold. It breaks open, birthing
worlds of new centers.

Eve Moore

Her eager spirit
devours her surroundings
turns them into poems.

Frances Benson

My book of notes—waits
to capture the tones and ticks
of my life. Or lives.

Jill Martindale Farrar

the healer is born
within the uterine walls
of the wound itself

Marsha Pincus

The words came out breech
Backwards, feet dangling, so she
Mid-wifed them around

Erika Hansen

we are born without
exoskeletons, creatures
of flesh, and deep bone

Eve Moore

situational
haiku he calls them I say
telling each piece true

Lisa Rizzo

Generosity
of spirit reigns in this place
Haiku Room refuge

Deb Cook

haiku masonry
building my world word by word
one small stone a time

Lisa Rizzo

black ribbon of ink
flowing mind to hand to page
tethers me to earth

Lisa Rizzo

Oh, seeds and cuttings
my gardening soul hungers
for rich, wormy soil

Deb Cook

her deft fingers dance
across warp and weft as they
spin ancient yarns

Marsha Pincus

Origami hands
will fold geometric words
into tiny cranes.

Lisa Sukenic

Words spark and ignite
tender tinder, dry fuel
strike a careful match.

Pam Helberg

Stark, spirited draft
and measured all-at-onceness.
Poem in a shot glass.

Jennifer Cool

this life a haiku
five steps forward then seven
steps backward repeat

Lisa Rizzo

fragmented pieces
crafted into mosaics
honor brokenness

Mary Pecaut

February

love

An early lover
reappears after decades
youth confronts old age.

Frances Benson

your stories can darn
her tapestry eaten by
moths of dementia

Marsha Pincus

As she smiles she bears
her teeth--part openness and
part fierce protection.

Frances Benson

What country would you
find if you traveled through the
atlas of my heart?

Pam Helberg

day one we opened
wide this room's door stepped inside
to greet each other

Lisa Rizzo

She couldn't recall the
precise moment her heart took
leave of her ribcage.

Ellen Tumavicus

our liquid lips sipped
each other for that first kiss
we remain unquenched

Liz Boquet

her body becomes
a bridge across his abyss
of silent longings

Marsha Pincus

he was a window
through him I saw otherness
then I saw myself

Jocelyn Rasmussen

Her dresses--skin tight
shoes with heels like skyscrapers
her heart--pure as snow.

Frances Benson

Play me for a fool
or like a Spanish guitar
my heart strings, your song.

Pam Helberg

20

she is a girl who
dreams of keys in love with a
boy who collects locks

Marsha Pincus

Words like locks tumbling
falling into place just so.
Speak the key to me.

Pam Helberg

Two chemtrails straddle
the moon near dawn, begging her
to penetrate him

Nance Broderzen

nestled between sheets
of paper their stories lie
In a lover's tryst

Marsha Pincus

remember lusting
in the box of your pickup
giddy stargazers

Jocelyn Rasmussen

she kisses her sweet
earth each evening 'fore turning;
her love's violet

Eve Moore

Child sleeps for two hours
Indecision taunts the air.
Sex, food, nap, or chores?

Mandy Brown

He goes to the gym,
takes our shrieking daughter too.
I re-fall in love.

Mandy Brown

In the dark, I wish
you could always touch me right
where I've been hurt most.

Kristen Ringman

the crumbs he's left for
her to follow were pieces
of her broken heart

Marsha Pincus

The dream of you is
heartbreakingly not the face
I see every day.

Kristen Ringman

She tucked her heart back
deep beyond her breast, her bones
and told it to stay

Nance Broderzen

he loved her even
more after she walked away
straight into his heart

Marsha Pincus

you cannot put a
splint on a heart if you are
the one who broke it

Marsha Pincus

now I will try to
give Echo back her body
write her flesh and bone

Marsha Pincus

love is the only
verb left after language is
annihilated

Marsha Pincus

24

She was a broken
human who used the jagged
shards to carve her way.

Sean Tribe

wishes liquefied
she poured hope to dull edges
in the wineglasses

Liz Boquet

my body is drawn
and quartered by the laser
gaze of his cold eyes

Marsha Pincus

kitchen wreckage states
last night's sworn testament in
dinner party dregs

Liz Boquet

your sharp edges once
sexy have not aged so well
you draw too much blood

Jocelyn Rasmussen

My ex still lives the
life I once had. I have less
now. I am free now.

Jenny Douglas

Catch and release these
vivid fantasies. Unhook,
swim fast, silver flash.

Pam Helberg

Deep bone chilling cold
The tangy scent of wood smoke
Opposites attract

Dori McCraw

his words like jazz so
unpredictable and fresh
my foot taps play me

Mary Pecaut

Grandpa's scythe sliced her
right arm off. With the left she
became a painter.

Jocelyn Rasmussen

your words chisel me
to pieces then mend me green
more whole than before

Mary Pecaut

"Legally binding!"
he likes to say, grinning wide,
farting profusely.

Rebecca Lovering Johnson

"Everything is a
Meditation," I muttered
As I ignored you.

Nicole Galland

I'm so much abler
than I thought before you said
I could be replaced.

Rebecca Lovering Johnson

Want to reach in and
fix the ear that twists words but
nothing can be done.

Rebecca Lovering Johnson

An itch I can't scratch
that's what you are, embedded
deep. Unreachable.

Pam Helberg

his crippled sermons
tilted windmillish toward her
root cellar reserves

Carrie Nassif

this expanding self,
yeast bubbled and foaming, it
gives itself away

Carrie Nassif

Do you still think I'm
amazing? Or now only
the sum of wrecked parts?

Kristen Ringman

she counts her faults like
beads on a rosary worn
smooth by her self doubts

Marsha Pincus

in our youth we played
in puddles rain in our hair
how dry we are now

Lisa Rizzo

cup your hands to hurt-
we know in our bones, our guts,
scar tissue is strength

Carrie Nassif

winter

To whom do you call?
Herald of the break of day
on this new crow morn.

Jennifer Newsome

Cinnamon rolls me
up in its hot, dough-sweet scent,
releases me, full.

Jennifer Steil

Hot flash makes it hard
to know if I am sweating
from yoga or age.

Jennifer Steil

Some write good stories
others look out the window
to see hot wet snow

Esther Cohen

Swiss snowflakes don't fall
they alight on chosen sites
divine precision

Liz Boquet

Speaking up and out
Moved by a sly archangel
Twirling on a branch.

Gillian Barlow

Wall frozen shadows
We hang between light and dark
Silent icicles.

Gillian Barlow

Wonderland of glass.
Crystal tears in glimmered drops.
Chandeliers in trees.

Lisa Lutwyche

A sanctuary
Not life apart, life itself
Enfolded this Room.

Erika Hansen

Deep freeze penetrates
Haunting shadows in the sun
Cold, crunching footsteps

Deb Cook

There wasn't a time
when she didn't think of words
parading in form.

Lisa Sukenic

Picturing the bulbs
bursting into wild, lush blooms
once Spring finds her path

Deb Cook

Daffodils pepper
a long-dead world, bulbs and roots
mingling like orgies.

Lisa Lutwyche

cows bow for thick licks
silver frosted field at dawn
grass popsicle treats

Liz Boquet

Horse's mane flying
freely, snow on branches dust
the blanket saddle.

Lisa Sukenic

sun melts glacial ice
river of grief swells, abates
cuts relief in stone

Mary Pecaut

sodden, the ground, where
tracks melt through the sucking thaw
like thumbpressed old flesh

Mil Norman-Risch

As the snow recedes,
my dog drapes herself on it
like a drunken tart.

Nicole Galland

Critter prints in snow
Devoured crab apples, proof of
Woodland bacchanal

Erika Hansen

April

faith

Inside your heart, do
you call yourself by the name
we know you, or more?

Teri Crane

"I shall build the world
with sparrow poems," she said.
"Let those who have ears..."

Mandy Brown

I am earth. I am
air. I am water. And pure
fire. I move with you.

Eve Moore

Every time she stood
up, the words came back into
her hands, writing grace.

Lisa Sukenic

Writing on whiteboards,
the squeaking of my knowledge
pours from hopeful hands.

Lisa Lutwyche

My words like wafers—
communion offered, received,
ingested. Some Truth.

Pam Helberg

Truth wants to vibrate
up and out in minor chords.
A sharp dissonance.

Pam Helberg

In his hoodlum youth,
searching for truth, he'd shoplift
books about karma.

Nicole Galland

So many metrics,
as though our souls' worth could be
captured by numbers.

Rebecca Lovering Johnson

Eyes closed I can make
my soul push against the skin
tight suit its wearing

Nance Broderzen

when daddy beat her
she rode on goddess wings and
swam with archetypes

Marsha Pincus

drilling through layers
of loss and failure she struck
a rich vein of faith

Jocelyn Rasmussen

blundering upward
she unfolds to this moment
it will prove enough

Lisa Rizzo

Nobody mentions
that a spider weaves her web
with blind leaps of faith.

Nicole Galland

The day's lesson? Joy.
It's teacher? Heartache. A long
dissonance training.

Jocelyn Rasmussen

how we are all leveled
to earth's surface
in proportion to the stars

Carrie Nassif

Can you let go of
what you're merely good at to
become your greatness?

Jocelyn Rasmussen

Arriving means the
chance of filling with light, not
the promise of sleep.

Sean Tribe

we are the stuff of
the stars; our birthright, if we
dare, is to burn bright

Eve Moore

The choir knows preaching
ain't good for much, no sir—song
is where the goods are.

Nicole Galland

snakeskinny dipping,
horse apples, and IEDs:
land mines in Eden.

Carrie Nassif

It's true, sometimes the
Hallelujah is broken.
But it's still holy.

Nicole Galland

Sometimes gratitude
expresses itself in sobs.
Words are just too small.

Nicole Galland

we'll go to Hell if
needed, but it's such a waste
of wings and wonder

Jocelyn Rasmussen

Scattering my words
like bird seed fertilizing
ground, new life begins.

Lisa Sukenic

May

spring

scores of starlings swoop
staccato notes punctuate
recapitulate

Mary Pecaut

Cardinal in the
crepe myrtle, squirrel's tail, geese
winging to high grass.

Pete Follansbee

Endless purple fields
where the hum of the bees fills
the lavender breeze.

Frances Benson

yellow butterfly
floated under redwood trees
just this—sufficient

Lisa Rizzo

Sitting in a bough
of camellia blossoms:
Floating in haiku.

Gillian Barlow

The screened in porch knew
no secrets to say it, now...
just the woven wind.

Lisa Sukenic

Tracing a message
Shadows dappling the lit wall
All-knowing tea tree.

Gillian Barlow

44

sun rich through new leaves
falls green and gold on warm skin
closed eyes open hands

Lisa Rizzo

lounging on chaise longue
spring's tender warmth envelops
growing going on

Liz Boquet

forsythia star
light shooting through the bleakness
make a wish for spring

Liz Boquet

Hushed rustle in night
Hastened bloom then retiring:
Pale shy moonflowers.

Gillian Barlow

Hyacinths planted
years long past have awakened
to bring joy today

Deb Cook

daffodils' bowed heads
rain pouring down their faces
listen, bright laughter

Lisa Rizzo

pitter patter quench
mud rows cup deep steeping wet
spring sips its field tea

Liz Boquet

garden's hung over
stupid tulips stayed open
all night rain drop shots

Liz Boquet

(Portuguese)
Amendoeiras
A saudade começa a
Renascer, em flor

(English)
Almond trees in bloom
The longing begins to be
Reborn, flowering

Erika Hansen

A five year old girl
what she was thankful for was
photosynthesis

Esther Cohen

If there were no words...?
(blade of grass held like a sword)
What then, grasshopper?

Gillian Barlow

I'm the wild spring winds
blowing apart my solid
state of delusion.

Eve Moore

June

family

Thinking in haiku
prompts people to ask why my
fingers are moving

Deb Cook

Sometimes I can't hold
back, I can't stop myself from
saying it all wrong.

Kristen Ringman

My eyes like apple
seeds newly planted with no
clue who'll stop and eat.

Sean Tribe

like so many stray
cats lost to human touch—our
abandoned stories

Mary Pecaut

How hard must I wish,
to conjure your words from air?
Eyes shut. Hands open.

Pam Helberg

Remember standing
on Cleveland St I have just
been told I'm pregnant.

Jill Martindale Farrar

There was no baby.
Only a pixel blizzard
on an ultrasound.

Jill Martindale Farrar

We rest inside the
wrinkles within Mother's palms.
Let us make few scars.

Mandy Brown

Bunnies sleep with her
tucked around her like an arm
because I'm not there.

Jennifer Steil

Like dust mote drifting
Buffeted by others breath
We inhabit dreams.

Gillian Barlow

First I was Alice,
then Marina, and then Red,
each girl loved, each lost.

Kristen Ringman

Raise your child as if
she will grow up to become
a famed memoirist.

Jennifer Steil

My first memory
is darkness, woods, a wolf,
a voice, and a scar.

Kristen Ringman

Women spun hens by
the neck. Quick death. My daughter
says I killed that quick.

Ruth Thompson

she will wear the scarf
knitted by Mother like a
cord wrapped round her neck

Marsha Pincus

in shadow I stay
no matter moonlight or clouds
beware my wolf-heart

Lisa Rizzo

Shunned by her child, the
mother cries out; others turn,
afraid it's catching.

Erika Hansen

Our reality

When combined with myth and hope
Creates great movies

Dori McCraw

My parent's house is
haunted. Each room—a vault of
ghosts wearing my clothes.

Kristen Ringman

fetally coiled;
martyrs, entangled among
unused safety nets

Carrie Nassif

you never forget
the feel of your father's fist
beating in your heart

Marsha Pincus

because her father
abandoned her she can love
with wild abandon

Marsha Pincus

Indigo griefs, old—
night's rainbows, like bruises bloom.
Once witnessed, loved, fade.

Tania Pryputniewicz

So long ago—you
say, eyes travel the ceiling
looking for the light.

Jill Martindale Farrar

Once I called him half-
brother; he said, "I'm a whole
person, your brother."

Erika Hansen

Fractious cat's paw tips
bottle to floor. Grandmother's
scent fills room. And soul.

Lisa Lutwyche

Our new capsized roles:
My children are parental
I baby my mum

Erika Hansen

July

summer

across dawn's bright moon
scoots one fleck, scoots another;
flocks scatter like stars

Carrie Nassif

Gentle dawn all pink
and blue with soft clouds floating
pretty atop trees.

Jennifer Newsome

words float hollow boned
settled for sleep, red birds wait
for morning's great O

Lisa Rizzo

if I say blue sky
if I say clear morning light
will you follow me?

Lisa Rizzo

Seven yellow birds
waving, crazily, in the
wind must mean something.

Lisa Lutwyche

cicada congress
drilling silence so loudly
blurring the message

Mary Pecaut

A red giant sun
will one day destroy the earth.
And still we write books.

Jennifer Steil

Crow flies too close, so
close that feathers scorched with pride
transform to shadow.

Jennifer Newsome

granite, bleached by sun,
pitted by tides, still surges
up to catch its breadth

Carrie Nassif

Crabs crawling from sand
awakening from their beds
of silver toned stones.

Sean Tribe

It's the tropics this
week. Let's keep Spanish hours, love,
and sleep through the heat.

Ruth Thompson

58

In the sweet perfume
of orange blossom honey,
sun and white flowers.

Jennifer Cool

The sun and moon meet
halfway through the sky tonight
for Equinox kiss.

Lisa Lutwyche

sadness can't withstand
chickadees in the birdbath
now splash in sunlight

Lisa Rizzo

Sunlight, without you
how would shadows dance when leaves
bob and bounce in wind?

Teri Crane

Following the light
The dog rotates on the rug
Like a sundial

Erika Hansen

Lion blonde the lawn
rayed by trees and boys at dusk
trading spines and manes.

Tania Pryputniewicz

Black-Eyed Susans nod
on nettled weedy wands: girls
strayed by wish and wind.

Tania Pryputniewicz

the goldfinch drabs in
sync with our sun's reach, as i
grow pale and dreamy

Eve Moore

Dandelion seeds
loosed from mystic's dream they drift,
our sons, to our bed.

Tania Pryputniewicz

I found a piece of
me in you full and ripe like
summer for harvest

Jocelyn Rasmussen

Husband splits oak rounds,
wife: carrots, sun's coins exchanged
by dusk: soup, firelight.

Tania Pryputniewicz

Again, the winds stir
fronds and old feelings. Debris.
By dusk we're left strewn.

Jennifer Cool

I'm so tired of this
lowering yellow-grey sky
dripping ennui. Drip.

Rebecca Lovering Johnson

A whole summer is
spent learning one lesson: to
let go when it's time.

Eve Moore

Touching the trees' bark
grounded in grassy damp earth
she feels the sunset

Nance Broderzen

and when the day stills,
squat sun spills off the pages,
writes her own ending

Carrie Nassif

Who can sing a swan
song but an ugly duckling
who survives changes?

Teri Crane

August

water

Composing haiku
counting heartbeats in shower
measuring my life.

Lisa Lutwyche

"Thunder is scary"
insists the little girl in
Amazon body.

Rebecca Lovering Johnson

Fear clutched me in bed
this morn, unknowns such a sea.
Then I heard the bird.

Jenny Douglas

Edges of a song
a shower of warm water on skin
nothing is silent.

Sean Tribe

Sun chases rain all
over sky, shakes cloud-glitter
on monkeypod trees.

Ruth Thompson

forecast's blunder slipped
mistook rain's claim on the day
mist took advantage

Liz Boquet

In truth, I love rain
for blessing my laziness
with holy water.

Nicole Galland

Cool cyclonic rain
falls on parched hot inland plain
desert garden smiles.

Jennifer Newsome

crackled ground resists
rain whose inky rivulets
batik my backyard

Carrie Nassif

Still the bush beckons
heavy drops on still parched plain
where clouds sweep grey hills.

Jennifer Newsome

raindrops splat windshield
street lights blue in water flicks
pollack painted glass

Mary Pecaut

they fall from my hands
with gratitude I bless them
back into the flow

Jocelyn Rasmussen

Brief rain like wind through
trees. Night moth against window:
patter of not-rain.

Ruth Thompson

Like-minded people
Watch ever-changing rivers
Through a sea of words

Dori McCraw

Fish flit and glisten
on the river's black surface
gulls swoop in and dine.

Frances Benson

well-worn river stones,
monotonous and skipping,
keep me from the shore

Carrie Nassif

Spring rain stipples lake.
Same sturgeon arc Mobius,
thrall to winter mind.

Tania Pryputniewicz

In the darkness of
the cave flows the river of
hope that soothes our souls.

Teri Crane

My sentences, like
wine. Drink from the blood rivers.
Exsanguination.

Pam Helberg

She planned to touch the
sun until discovering
depths in the ocean.

Teri Crane

Grey ocean water
churning shoreward resonates
primal energy

Deb Cook

waves fold sea to shore —
shore to sea — smooth blue creases
liquid ironing

Liz Boquet

Sea's spindle spools tight
the dress I fell asleep in.
Which moved? Hem or shore?

Tania Prypniewicz

The tide crashes forth
retreats, crashes her 'til she
stands knee deep in sand

Nance Broderzen

While bobbing on the
surface, something slithers by
my bare, dangling legs.

Sean Tribe

Clouds swam in today,
big sea turtles over reef:
me in fish traffic.

Ruth Thompson

In dreams my selkie-
skin, such tender seaweed, comes
home around my bones.

Ruth Thompson

They say you can band
them then—sitting on eggs, deep
dream, eyes blind with sky.

Ruth Thompson

sea sheet of iron
dimpled by day's fingertips
dance what sky commands

Lisa Rizzo

One day, the sea spit
me out like a cork, but it
choked on my heart strings.

Kristen Ringman

Take heart. Water is
no good at remembering
how to become ice.

Jennifer Cool

71

September

fall

Autumn sky streaked grey
and purple and orange as
sunset summons us

Deb Cook

Muted, edgeless clouds
Light and dark, like bone and air
Heaven's vertebrae

Erika Hansen

Autumn air sharpens,
crisping silhouettes, sunlight
while I slow, soften.

Jennifer Steil

Pale mauve sky through ferns
aching silent rain forest—
Find the words. Say it.

Jill Martindale Farrar

the ticking crickets
serenade the harvest moon
counting down to fall

Marsha Pincus

Last light pinks the sky,
early. Stark branches, nearly
leafless, shrug, resigned.

Lisa Lutwyche

So Fall has fallen.
Now we slouch toward leaflessness
and fractal branches.

Nicole Galland

Winds flog the thinning
trees, sending yellow pools to
their sad, swaying feet.

Lisa Lutwyche

My red umbrella
blew to bits in the storm—now
just bare maple tree.

Nicole Galland

Lost branches, we stand
like trees, mangled by hard winds.
Our roots deepen us.

Nance Broderzen

Simmering beneath
the forest's floor, a thousand
seeds fracture for life.

Lisa Lutwyche

A plant with a tap
root, a so-called weed, she grows
downward to survive.

Erika Hansen

In cool of evening,
chill of coming winter creeps
into my garden.

Jennifer Newsome

One bright path emerged
in the darkened forest, but
he tripped over it.

Teri Crane

Ah memory, come
to me, bring me your pods with
strong-scented songs.

Jill Martindale Farrar

October

world

Small world wisdom. Stop.
Write the madness out of you.
Then it will be still.

Lisa Sukenic

New kind of quiet
not understanding the words
that spew forth in French.

Frances Benson

I envy the sloth
his genetic excuses
to ignore the clock.

Mandy Brown

The brandy slid down
consolingly as Alice
down the rabbit hole.

Jill Martindale Farrar

A wedding gown floats,
deep in Lake Ontario,
a jilted bride's dress.

Lisa Sukenic

she's walked the past so
often she has made trenches
in the ground of time

Marsha Pincus

Lexicographic
codes leaving no stone unturned,
a fossil imprint.

Lisa Sukenic

Pouring paths today.
 Window music: slump-crunch of
concrete, shovel shove.

Ruth Thompson

Tongan master rock
wall builder chips lava, fits
 each to the next. Sings.

Ruth Thompson

The workers next door,
wrecking my health and mind, build
a wellness center.

Jennifer Steil

The pigeon man sat
birds perched on shoulders just like
clothespins on a line.

Lisa Sukenic

We were too wild, too
enraptured for their liking.
I lament their chains.

Kristen Ringman

The call-help button
near the elevator door
is worn smooth. Breathe deep.

Frances Benson

With two raised eyebrows
he invited me right in
to his racism.

Erika Hansen

Every Sunday night
just around this very time
my week glides right by

Esther Cohen

Fainted at the gym.
Two men ignored me, one man
denounced my bare feet.

Jennifer Steil

In my home country,
each downcast pair of eyes looks
for what they can't have.

Kristen Ringman

He hands me the news
as if it's something that will
lift me from the gloom.

Jennifer Steil

I can't read the news
and believe it wise to trust
the world with my child.

Jennifer Steil

"I don't have baggage,"
She protested too loudly.
"I have memories."

Jennifer Steil

would I were a sieve,
sifting judgment's brackish grey
while panning for bold

Carrie Nassif

She invents a place,
a country of her own, says
we can't get visas.

Jennifer Steil

Old explorers know
all maps are a fantasy.
Terra firmament.

Jennifer Cool

I can't possibly
travel far enough away
from where I grew up.

Kristen Ringman

A map of the world
fills me with wanderlust. The
Levant has long arms.

Deb Cook

I could live in an
airport, watching people move,
cultures meeting there.

Kristen Ringman

Now they smell even
more like me—cave, dream, whale-fall,
old bones. My spice road.

Ruth Thompson

Along the Spice Route
Ancient civilizations
Invite myth and awe

Deb Cook

when the elephants
tromp, the fog descends, and the
street signs read backwards

Eve Moore

I left my heart on
the streets of South India,
broken and lonely.

Kristen Ringman

I am nostalgic
for everywhere I have been
except here and now.

Jennifer Steil

November

night

We will sleep in the
nest, like birds in twigs, fastened
together with twine.

Lisa Sukenic

Crisp cool night touches
me through the screen, delicate
moth wings, rice paper.

Lisa Sukenic

Nights like this your words
arrived on moonbeams, dancing—
spinning into me.

Pam Helberg

Back to back we sleep
two halves of one butterfly
shared thorax of dreams.

Tania Pryputniewicz

If I'd ink to spill
I'd spill it on you, and write
you into the stars.

Nicole Galland

just one break in clouds
unleashes galaxy of
dancing stars on lake

Mary Pecaut

thank you the woman
said to the girl still inside
for dreaming these dreams

Marsha Pincus

Night's obsidian!
Velvet lives I long to try,
one redwing blackbird.

Tania Pryputniewicz

My mantra: release.
Bird cries in the still green air.
Be still my heart. Still.

Jill Martindale Farrar

frogs sing semitones
night sky winks through scrim of clouds
bats choreograph

Jocelyn Rasmussen

Bats silhouetted
gliding, seeking silently
early morning moon.

Jennifer Newsome

day can't unbutton
tucked in too tight into night
sleep with one eye closed

Liz Boquet

Nightmares are only
the earth sighing from the cold
embrace of matter.

Sean Tribe

Dreams, insights, gut-calls
Our cellular memory
Bids us to listen

Deb Cook

inky brackish chill
night, a predator pupil
ponderous and still

Carrie Nassif

Ghost wind all night slams
invisible doors, keyholes
skinny rain fingers.

Ruth Thompson

Not quite a full moon
lies at highway's end like a
goblin's head, rolling...

Lisa Lutwyche

I want to be brave
for me, for you—kneel in the
dark for the bold shoes.

Jenny Douglas

Silence spirals up
rising like the heat of a
clarifying fire.

Pam Helberg

Fireplace draws, though green-
vined. Once mynahs lived inside,
talked story at night.

Ruth Thompson

Night. The snow whispers
laying a blanket of, "Hush,"
on the modern world.

Lisa Lutwyche

Like sump pumps in a
basement, roots draw winter's melt
in: testing the pipes.

Pete Follansbee

I can't keep birthing
words into silence. These are
boisterous children.

Pam Helberg

The moon jellyfish
Boneless, brainless, heartless; they
Know how to survive.

Erika Hansen

Large moon's slow ascent
Arcs overhead—leaning in
Desires earth's closeness.

Gillian Barlow

Clouds silent as dusk
brush nectar-colored walls warm
with incandescence.

Jill Martindale Farrar

Artemis rose full
I followed her white dress caught
in night's grassy field

Lisa Rizzo

90

If an instrument
the harp, unplucked, strung and tuned
gowned girl is veiled moon.

Tania Pryputniewicz

The scent of the night
like sea, like sorrow, like stone,
releases memories.

Jennifer Steil

We dwell here between
words, beyond voice, in this our
violent silence.

Pam Helberg

Your silence echoes
through my canyons of desire—
freshly gouged and deep.

Pam Helberg

November Thursday
long full day of blue moments
wrote forgiveness poem

Esther Cohen

Tonight's moon laments,
"No one ever loved me best."
"There's time," I tell her.

Jennifer Cool

December

endings

once upon a time
happily ever after
wasn't the ending

Eve Moore

Winter's bite returns
Sharp teeth pierce the day's brightness
Her time's not up yet

Deb Cook

my mother lies frail
fully pregnant with dying
last delivery

Mil Norman-Risch

"She's gone," I told him.
No answer. An hour passes.
"Wait and see," he said.

Mil Norman-Risch

to die in the dark
is a fine death; nobody
checking: "is it yet?"

Mil Norman-Risch

I can't say the words
"My brother and sister died"
But I can write them.

Erika Hansen

Father, you held us
together with the pieces
of mothers who died.

Kristen Ringman

he carves the coffin
with the same steady hands he used
to carve the cradle

Marsha Pincus

I'd like to find you
before I'm ashes and dust,
before the fire's snuffed.

Jocelyn Rasmussen

But to die is hard
To leave behind all those un-
ticked boxes. Un-done.

Jill Martindale Farrar

Sometimes I miss him
dead so long before he died
so long alone now

Nance Broderzen

He loved to-do lists.
And now, with efficiency
He had checked off death.

Erika Hansen

Fetal position
Cramps, bloating, and body aches
Winter is coming.

Mandy Brown

Pain must be trying
to teach me something crucial,
something I don't learn.

Jennifer Steil

The words are fading,
condensation on foggy
pane, I trace what's left.

Lisa Sukenic

Things only we knew.
Now you're gone, I'm condemned to
know it all alone.

Nicole Galland

at death our flesh turns
into words those who love us
whisper to themselves

Marsha Pincus

Which face do I have?
Which life am I allowed to
build from his absence?

Kristen Ringman

Phones around me beep
like the life support machines
that warn us of death.

Jennifer Steil

It's all amazing
When you know you'll be leaving.
We are all leaving.

Ellen Tumavicus

How long will it be,
she asked, before we are dust
and we feed the trees?

Jennifer Steil

She talked to the dead
and the wind howled through the lips
of her steel canteen

Nance Broderzen

'Killing is easy,'
says Genet. The heart opens
and awaits the knife.

Jill Martindale Farrar

she would kill him off
with the stroke of a pen if
she thought he'd stay dead

Marsha Pincus

Your handwriting cuts
my heart. I crawl inside each
loop and dash, and cry.

Erika Hansen

Here lie the ashes
Personal body remains
I do not live here

Dori McCraw

Scatter my ashes
from a hot air balloon, wear
lipstick and a hat.

Erika Hansen

Blood of my blood, how
I wish I'd seen your face, eyes
feet, limbs. Mysteries!

Jill Martindale Farrar

In my last hours, may
you remember my love a
thousand kisses deep.

Jill Martindale Farrar

This year has ended
endings and beginnings now
are often the same

Esther Cohen

CONTRIBUTORS

GILLIAN BARLOW

Too few syllables
to say what it is I want—
writer not poet

FRANCES BENSON

She is a woman
of few words which is why she
likes to write haiku

LIZ BOQUET

Watchmaker's wife writes
about wishes and wonders
abracadabra

NANCE BRODERZEN

Years of digging through
foundations to source fuel her
pen flights from L.A.

MANDY BROWN

Spinning in stillness,
she hears moments of caught breath
to trap on the page.

ESTHER COHEN

I'm Esther Cohen
sometimes red-headed, curly
rent-stabilized home.

DEB COOK

Sixty-six years in
just seventeen syllables
leave me wanting more

JENNIFER COOL

Jenny Cool's her name,
born in light but lives in shame,
for want of writing.

TERI CRANE

Educator, crone,, no sir
hint of mirth, dash of steadfast,
optimist, helper.

104

JENNY DOUGLAS

Curious gypsy
happy to join you here, now.
We'll sit and drink tea.

JILL MARTINDALE FARRAR

Poet, troubadour
word detective, thief: I write
right where the heart glows

PETE FOLLANSBEE

Pete Follansbee, a
teacher and haiku friend from
Richmond, Virginia.

NICOLE GALLAND

Day job: Novelist.
Night job: Insomniac who
started Haiku Room.

ERIKA HANSEN

Married with two kids
and a dog in the heartland.
Who would have thunk it?

PAM HELBERG

Pam's a therapist-
in-training. Also—writer,
mother, black sheep, friend.

REBECCA LOVERING JOHNSON

Spirited talker,
linguistics student, writer,
words are my business.

LISA LUTWYCHE

Mother, Wife, Poet:
paints watercolors, teaches,
rescues cats—inspires.

DORI MCCRAW

Adult only child
with an only child brother.
Parents encouraged.

EVE MOORE

a bee, I sip this
bloom, that, conjugating wild
worlds of consciousness

CARRIE NASSIF

therapist/poet
luring the "I" of her swarm
from it's tiny cage

JENNIFER NEWSOME

Of the music's muse
tending gardens of delight
viewed through archer's sight

MIL NORMAN-RISCH

Grown from good seeds, she
saw green leaves become mothwings:
Mind's fresh motherings.

MARY PECAUT

Writes prose to under-
stand self, composes poems
to clarify life.

MARSHA PINCUS

She taught others to
write for thirty-five years but
now she writes herself

TANIA PRYPUTNIEWICZ

With love, gratitude,
a feral emissary
of our haiku heart.

JOCELYN RASMUSSEN

singer-songwriter
composes in seventeen
syllable measure

KRISTEN RINGMAN

Wild. Poet. Runner.
Novelist. Mermaid. Mother.
Sailor. deaf. Nomad.

LISA RIZZO

this poet teaches
travels wide gatherings words
shaped into poems

JENNIFER STEIL

International
woman of mystery who
writes fiction and non.

LISA SUKENIC

Writer, poet, kid
lit. I teach, I speak, charge ions,
zap those around me.

RUTH THOMPSON

Silenced, I broke free.
Earth's body brought me home. Now,
late poet, sing Yes!

SEAN TRIBE

Traveling to find
new ghosts to give mine new dreams
to help me sleep.

ELLEN TUMAVICUS

Art teacher for dough,
artist for substance, mother
for sugar and spice.

112

www.ingramcontent.com/pod-product-compliance
Lightning Source LLC
Chambersburg PA
CBHW032042040426
42449CB00007B/988